THERE IS HOPE

LETTERS TO MY YOUNG BROTHERS!

Richard D. Terrell

Letters to My Young Brothers: There is Hope!

ISBN: 979-8-9923794-3-3

Contact Richard D. Terrell at www.mrrichardterrell.com for school visits, speaking engagements, freelance projects, and interviews.

This book was inspired by my
eldest son, Zyree.

Thank you for your inspiration.

You are amazing just the way you are.

Remember, always put God first and
believe in yourself.
Love you always.

This book is dedicated to my
young brother,
Robert D. Terrell
1/18/1989 - 12/5/2024

TABLE OF CONTENTS

DEDICATION

This book is dedicated to all my young brothers regardless of background, race, religion, class and/or culture.

For those of you who have dreamed to do great things, who are currently doing great things, and who are planning to do even greater things.

For you who are feeling lost in this journey we call life.

For you who feel as if no one cares about you and the things you are going through right now.

For you who are aspiring to be the next great leader for yourself, your family, your community, and the world.

For you that has been discouraged due to others speaking down at you.

For you that have been living day-to-day, trying to live in the moment and enjoy life's daily accomplishments.

For you that wake up in the morning and turn on the TV and notice someone else getting killed due to senseless violence—black-onblack crime or a police officer killing another unarmed black young man.

For you that have struggled with self-awareness, self-identity, and/or self-love. This book is for **YOU!**

INTRODUCTION

I am happy and honored that you have decided to give this book a chance. It has been a very long time coming. I should have written this book a few years ago, but you and I both know that life can get in the way. Sometimes distractions come. Sometimes you have to go through some things. However, when you get on the other side—when you make it through—you are stronger and can touch more people through your testimony by sharing your story.

Because of what I've been through and my many downfalls, there were times I wanted to give up and not face life with a different mindset (a growth mindset) and a new perspective. Now, I would say that this book has the power to potentially change, shape, and/or build your life.

This book is organized by letters that I have written to you. After each letter, I will propose a question, so you have a chance to physically respond to what I have shared in the letter. Those questions are good discussion points to share with your family and friends.

For me, writing is a very therapeutic option that allows me to share my thoughts. Through my writing, I am able to find my voice when I feel voiceless.

It is my hope that by actively engaging and responding to the challenged questions, writing will be a therapeutic avenue to help you find your voice the same way I found mine.

Enjoy each question and be honest with your responses. Honesty is the key to understanding yourself more, expecting more from who you are, and moving forward in your journey.

You can choose to write the response on the page given (which I would highly encourage you to do), or you will also have the opportunity to send me that response via email. My email address is: mrrichardterrell@gmail.com. If you decide to send me an email, I promise I will respond to you in a timely fashion, and we can start a dialogue between the two of us.

During the process of writing this book, my desire is to: **CHALLENGE, INSPIRE, EMPOWER, MOTIVATE,** and **ENCOURAGE** you.

There are many reasons why you are reading this book. One of the reasons, maybe because:

1. You probably know me as Mr. Terrell because I currently work at the school you are attending or have worked at a school you attended.
2. You probably have heard me speak at your school, a community event, or your church.
3. You received this book as a gift and someone thought you would like it.
4. You like reading books that are different.
5. You heard that it was a good read.
6. The front cover seemed very interesting, so you are giving this book a chance.
7. You are reading it because you were inspired by something I said or posted on social media.
8. You are reading it because a father, mother, uncle, brother, or sister, etc. challenged you.
9. You are reading it because you are bored and have nothing else to do.
10. You are reading it because you want to become a better young man.

11. If you are reading it for some other reason, please write it down:

_____

_____

_____

_____

_____

_____

_____

_____

No matter the reason you are reading this, I appreciate you for that.

Before you start reading the enclosed letters, let me share with you the reason why I named this book *There is Hope: Letters to My Young Brothers.*

Growing up, the only thing that kept me grounded and focused was having "hope" and seeing beyond what was going on in my life at that moment. We know that sometimes life doesn't always go as planned or what we have envisioned. As a young man growing up, creating and fulfilling goals, and dreaming about a better tomorrow, a better week, a better month, and perhaps a better year. That is hope!

What is HOPE?

For me, hope is having the growth mindset and the optimism to look towards your greater future than your current situation.

For example:
It was the summer of 2001, the summer before entering my freshman year of high school. I was playing football for a local recreational center in South Minneapolis called Powderhorn Park; the football season was going great. We were competing at a high level and were winning most of our games. Our brotherhood and bond were unbreakable. We were doing our thing. In fact, we got into the playoffs and won the semifinals. The championship game was played at the former Minnesota Vikings stadium, the Metrodome.

The night before the game, our coach had us practice in the rain, and it literally poured down raining that evening. We were somewhat upset due to the rain and yet excited for the opportunity to play in the stadium. Looking back, our hope was to practice very hard and to prepare ourselves for the victory against one of our rival teams, Dr. Martin Luther King, Jr. Park. During the practice, we ran differently and we spoke to each other differently; everything was different about that practice compared to practices during the season.

The hope in that moment was there! Hoping that this intense practice would pay off. Hoping that everything would come together and fulfill everyone's dream of being a champion. The growth mindset and the optimism were very high.

The next day (game day) we got on the field with the same momentum that we practiced with the night before. Ready to compete! Ready to go at it with King Park. We were ready!

Unfortunately, we lost the game by one point. At that moment, we were very upset and disappointed. We felt defeated. We felt like our hard work the day before didn't pay off. Thinking back, it truly makes me smile because it showed how passionate we were, preparing for that big game. Despite the loss, our hope grew a little stronger that day.

Just know, I am not perfect. I do not consider myself an expert. I do struggle. I am currently working on some things as I am writing this. I firmly believe my passion and personal story of overcoming life's obstacles will help guide the next generation of leaders. I am doing this to help you become more aware of the things in your life, so that you do not fall in the same trap that I did.

Please take full advantage of the knowledge and literature in these letters. This book, and the letters in it, will definitely touch your mind, body, and soul, but only if you allow it to.

I hope that this book touches you like it touched me as I am writing these letters to you.

You got this!
Richard D. Terrell

YOU ARE SMART

My definition of SMART

Sophisticated

Mysterious

Acceptable

Rare

Talented

Letter 1

WHY ME?

"Consider thinking and asking, "Why not me?" Instead of asking, "Why me?"

-Richard D. Terrell-

Dear Young Brother,

This is my first letter to you. I am happy that I was given this opportunity to write to you.

I am currently in downtown Minneapolis, Minnesota waiting for my next client to arrive. I often drive for Lyft. I drive to earn some extra money, socialize with individuals I don't know, and think and process things, such as writing through this letter. I can start complaining and questioning things about driving for Lyft, but I'm not. There is no need to do that. In one of my favorite movies, *The Great Debaters*, one of the actors said, "We do what we have to do in order to do what we want to do." I constantly say that to myself when I am driving for Lyft. Instead of asking, "Why me?" I just simply say, "Why not me?"

You are probably thinking to yourself, *"Why did he start with the question, Why me?"* I know this question can be answered in many ways depending on how you think about it. Considering this, I would like for you to look at the bigger picture.

Oftentimes, I thought to myself, *Why me? Why did I have to go through many trials and tribulations to get to where I am now? Why did I have to deal with many issues, consequences, and problems in my life? Why couldn't I have a normal life? What is a normal life?* Young brother, I too have been through many things in my life and have questioned, *Why me?*

I would like to share a few things that I've asked myself before coming to better understand this journey we call life:

Why did I have to grow up in a single-parent household?

Why was my father absent for the majority of my life?

Why did I have to go into foster care due to my mother's addictions growing up?

Why did my grandparents raise my siblings and I?

Why did I grow up fighting all the time for no reason?

Why did I get kicked out of school for fighting, acting up, and other behavioral issues leading me to attend an alternative school?

Why did I not care about my education while I was in high school?

Why did I lose my scholarship because my GPA (Grade Point Average) was 0.07 after my first year of college? Yes, I did! The only class I passed was gym, and that was with a D (don't laugh).

Why did I struggle in school?

Why did I change my college program so many times?

Why did I blame others for my own doing?

Why did I not love myself enough to control my actions and behavior?

Why did I not take some of my friendships and relationships more seriously?

Why did I use some people to get what I wanted in life?

Why did I not manage my finances correctly?

Why?

These are just a few of the questions I have asked, and there are many more which I will share with you later on. You may have your own questions, and that's okay. Just make sure that you arenot playing the blame game. Everything that we go through is for a reason. There is a lesson in it all, even if at that very moment we do not know what for.

You see, we all have to go through things in order to become special and unique. I had to and still go through many things in order to be able to write this book for you. I've passed and failed many life tests, but the challenge is to not give up.

Back in 2013, I had the greatest opportunity to attend a Young Preachers Conference in Atlanta, GA, where I was able to share my story with others. While I was there, a pastor was teaching about forgetting about the past, moving forward, and walking in your purpose. During his lecture, he asked everyone the question "Why not you?" It was very interesting that he asked that because prior to the workshop, some other young preachers and I were having a conversation. We were all curious about why God called us to do His work. After the conference, I told myself, "I am done asking the question, 'Why me?'" I also understood that sometimes things happen to make you a better individual.

You may have low points in your life when you question everything. This is when the "Why me?" question will come in. These low points may be small or large and life-altering, but with every fall, have the strength to get back up, because the world still goes on. When you stand back up after falling, it is called a *breakthrough*.

One of my low points in life was when I entered foster care as a young man. Thankfully, I was placed in the home of my grandparents, but I still struggled. I fought with others throughout my childhood—in school and my neighborhood. Because of that, I was transferred from a public elementary school to an alternative school—basically a school for students who had behavioral issues.

The stigma that as a black boy you are either going to end up in jail or six feet under is truly harsh. Throughout my youth, I knew I would be somebody regardless of some of the wrong turns I took early on. I wanted something different for myself. I wanted to break generational curses. I wanted to be the first in my family to do something while continuing my family's great legacy.

Why Not Me? My mother is a strong black woman who got on her feet and truly makes me proud. She continues to fight every single day to be happy by leading others at her place of employment and building stronger relationships with her children and grandchildren. My grandmother is a powerful Christian woman. Growing up, I witnessed her taking care of our family (opening her home for others to live there) and working a full-time job. Then when my grandfather got sick, she was there right by his side caring for him and making sure he was comfortable. She fought through cancer during the summer of 2018, which was definitely a scary moment for the family. She is a true example of a fighter despite anything that goes on with life. My late grandfather was a father figure to me and countless people who really needed it growing up. God rest his soul.

I have a wonderful support system (family, close friends, and my brothers of Alpha Phi Alpha Fraternity, Inc.) right beside me that continues to encourage me when I feel unworthy. I have a community of believers who keep me accountable, even when I don't feel like listening to them speaking their truth about what I am doing or what is going on. I have mentors who I can talk to when things do not seem to be working for my good and when things get tough.

Regardless of what society says about African American young men, I indeed graduated from high school on time, attended college, graduated from college, and also went on to attend two graduate programs to get my Master's degrees.

I have no excuses!

Young brothers, you are here for a reason. You are here to do something great and to do something that will not only benefit you but your family, your community, and the world. Once you realize that, everything you've been through, are going through, and will go through will only make you a stronger and wiser individual. Your past issues, problems, consequences, and behavior are only a stepping stone for the greater, which is to come. Look at it as though you and only you went through these obstacles. You have to share it with the world so they understand that your current and future happiness did not come overnight and you had to work very hard to get past life's obstacles.

So, stop asking, "Why me?" and start saying, *"Why not me?"*

My challenge question to you:

Why not you?

_____

_____

_____

_____

_____

_____

_____

_____

_____

_____

_____

_____

_____

_____

_____

Remember, you can email me your response at mrrichardterrell@gmail.com.

To you, my young brother.
Richard D. Terrell

Letter 2

WHAT IS YOUR PURPOSE?

"Your purpose comes from within."

-Richard D. Terrell-

Dear Young Brother,

This is my second letter to you. I hope all is well with you and yours, and that you are doing great wherever you are while reading this letter. Maybe you're at school, work, the recreation center, or just chilling and relaxing at home.

I'm currently working through this letter and watching my local news station, WCCO. I have to be honest with you, I am emotional and heartbroken at the moment because of what I just saw in the news. I just heard about eighteen young people (particularly black and brown young men and women) were recently arrested and indicted for some overnight crimes in downtown Minneapolis, Minnesota. Those crimes include assault, theft, etc. I wondered to myself, *What are they doing downtown at 4 a.m.? What stores or restaurants are open around that time? Simply why?* I then realized that those young people and other young people across the country in the inner cities are dealing with idle/free time.

They need positive guidance, support, more structure, and love from the community. I ended my thoughts with, *What can I do to help my community?*

In this letter, I want to share the importance of finding and understanding your purpose.

What is your purpose?

This question is another unique question that I tend to ask young people that I speak with. Sometimes you look all over to find your true purpose in life. You might look on social media, television, or at individuals you look up to like rappers or professional athletes.

Please understand that your purpose does not come from those things. They can be your motivation, your drive, or the reason why you are doing that certain thing in life. Your true purpose comes from within—meaning your purpose comes from your heart. Things that you have a great passion for, things that keep you happy and excited about getting up in the morning.

My purpose kept changing as I looked externally to fill it. I was the one who looked at things and would say to myself, "I think I can do this or I think I can do that." During my years in college, I changed my major many times throughout my six years in undergraduate school. (A major is the area you plan to specialize in college).

My major went from Sociology to International Affairs. I then changed it to Business Management, and then again to Business Administration. I eventually declared my major in Communications with a focus on Journalism and graduated with a Bachelor of Science in it. I declared Journalism as a focus because I always enjoyed writing. During those years of transition, my area of focus changed a lot because I thought my purpose in life was different than it really is.

While I was in high school, I wanted to be a lawyer and pursue a degree to practice law in the State of Minnesota. For many years, I thought that was my purpose so I lived law; I worked at a law firm in downtown Minneapolis, MN for seven summers (I will share that story in a later letter). I talked about law by sharing with others because I wanted to pursue a law degree. I even studied law on my own by researching and understanding the various law statutes and regulations.

But it was in the fall of 2012 that I fully received a word from God to accept the calling to ministry. I felt God speaking to my heart to focus more on community, education, and activism with youth, family, and community outreach. This way, I would focus on educating youth, young adults, and families on various issues such as spirituality, education, life, family, and community. Hearing from God and receiving various signs from him helped me to see my purpose. This excites my heart! This is what I have a passion for! This is what I stay up all night thinking about. This makes me happy!

Fast forward to 2019. My resume is filled with many employers, educational institutions I have attended, many accolades, the starting of my own business, and the different roles I have pursued in ministry.

You will come to realize in your journey of life that you will not have one purpose on earth. You will not have only one objective. You will be forever changing goals, pursuing goals, working on goals, or letting goals go.

The saying some people come into your life for a reason, season, or lifetime is similar to your purpose. There's a reason why you have ups and downs or obstacles; you're being prepared for further growth. Sometimes you will encounter such things as meeting someone in the field you enjoy and having the opportunity to learn a little bit more and be mentored.

You will experience many seasons for your purpose—some long and some short. You will find joy in what you are doing. You will be sharing your talents and living in your purpose will ultimately continue your growth as a young man into manhood.

Your experiences in this part of your life will educate you further and provide flight to the possibility of your next purpose in life.

Your purpose will make a foundation for you, your family, and others who are in your life. The growth you have experienced in the reason and season stage, will be with you for a lifetime and shape who you are due to the many lessons you have learned.

Right now, you may or may not know your purpose in life. That is okay. That is exactly what I intended to help you find.

First, find your purpose.

Second, understand your purpose.

Lastly, walk in your purpose.

Finding your Purpose!

Finding your purpose takes dedication, commitment, and can come with some challenges. One must understand who you rely on when things get tough. For me, it is God, who I confess is my Lord and Savior.

To find your purpose, seek forth understanding through prayer.

One of my favorite scriptures in the bible comes from Jeremiah 29:11 (NKJV). "For I know the thoughts that I think toward you, says the Lord, thoughts of peace and not of evil, to give you a future and a hope." I love this passage because the author, Jeremiah, speaks about his love for the people in Jerusalem; at the time, the people were going through crises that caused them to think negatively about their future. Jeremiah shared with them what the Lord spoke to him about. Sometimes, I feel negative or separated about my future, and honestly, I feel this about my present. So, I often think about the story of Jeremiah and his people, and that scripture gives me a sense of hope and confidence.

This step will take weeks, months, or even years. There are times when God will put you through certain things to see how committed you are to knowing Him and knowing your purpose in life. This is alright! You got this! He will show you that you must submit solely to Him and lean not on your own doing and understanding.

Understanding your Purpose!

As I shared above, my passion and love is for youth, families, and the community. I have to be honest; it took me many years to understand that and to see what God had been showing me all those years. I have worked at various recreational centers, schools, and various other places. While working at those schools and recreational centers, I was always given an opportunity to meet with young men to mentor and coach them through their journey. Mentoring and coaching came very easily for me. That is what I was happy doing. I woke up every day excited to pour life into the young men. I shared my story; I heard their stories, and we worked together on many projects.

Understanding your purpose takes a different kind of commitment and dedication. This commitment and dedication come from you. How committed are you to understanding your purpose?
Are you ready to go through the fight? It is mental, emotional, and sometimes even physical.

Understanding your purpose comes in various ways in life. You may get an opportunity to work somewhere new. You may get an opportunity with a new person. You may get the opportunity to teach someone a skill you have not perfected. During this process of understanding your purpose, be on the lookout for opportunities that come your way. The doors they open may lead to enhancing your purpose. Even to this day, I am still cultivating my purpose through attending conferences, meeting with individuals in the field, and doing my own research. Just make sure you are working through it day by day. It is definitely a process.

Walking in your Purpose!

Walking in your purpose gives you the opportunity to share your gift and talent with others. Serving others in a different way that brings you happiness is truly walking in your purpose. I like what the Late Dr. Martin Luther King, Jr said in two of his quotes,

"Whatever your life's work is, do it well. A man should do his job so well that the living, the dead, and the unborn could do it no better."

"If a man is called to be a street sweeper, he should sweep streets even as Michelangelo painted, how Beethoven composed music, or how Shakespeare wrote poetry. He should sweep streets so well that all the hosts of heaven and earth will pause to say, here lived a great street sweeper who did his job well."

I know what you are thinking about the second quote, "I don't want to be a street sweeper." Dr. King was basically saying: Do it great! Do it with love! Do it with passion! Do it unconditionally! Do it with no limits! Do it with no excuses! Do it with your heart! Put your blood, sweat, and tears in it. While doing it, you will feel wonderful about your work. Whatever you are called to do and what your purpose in life is, do it well! Others will see that you are happy with what you are doing and that you are truly walking in your purpose.

Don't cling to a dream if it is the wrong dream, even if you have spent a lot of time cultivating it. The moment you recognize you are called to something else, be willing to move on. If we all clung to the idea of what we said we were going to be when we were in kindergarten, we'd all be off track because our dreams grow and mature with us. I would be a basketball player if I could have the dream of my youth. I had skills too, but an injury on the court took that dream away from me. My dreams adjusted and became more fine-tuned as I grew. Yours will too.

Be open to change. Change is scary and getting out of your comfort zone is even scarier, but that first step will open more doors imaginable when leading to your purpose. Know that when you are challenging yourself or being challenged by others, your purpose driven life will be fruitful. Continue to be open to new possibilities and when you hear you can do all things, believe it.

Do not end up at a dead end. The reason why people reach a dead end and stay there is because they have lost hope. A dead end is when someone has decided to stay where they are rather than looking inward. They have given up on themselves. It is when they have decided they will try no other paths out of the fear of the unknown. Instead of living for their purpose, they are settling for what is comfortable. Do not lose hope. Greater things will come to those who keep going, keep fighting, and keep thriving.

Find your purpose!
Understand your purpose!
Walk in your purpose!
Go for it! You got this!

My challenge question to you:

Where does your happiness come from?

_____

_____

_____

_____

_____

_____

_____

_____

_____

_____

_____

_____

_____

_____

Remember, you can email me your response to mrrichardterrell@gmail.com.

To you, my young brother.
Richard D. Terrell

Letter 3

LEARN SOMETHING NEW EVERYDAY!

"Every day is a new day to learn something new."

-Richard D. Terrell-

Dear Young Brother,

This is my third letter to you. I hope things are going great for you and that you are enjoying this book. I also hope you are learning something that will help you through this journey we call life.

I'm currently sitting at my oldest son, Zyree's football practice watching him, which I often do. Zyree has been playing for the same football team for the last five years. I learned something very interesting this football season about him. Prior to today, before each game, while driving to the field, I would help him prepare. I would turn on some rap and/or hip-hop music so it can get him hyped up, turn it up, and lit, and ready for the game. I would try to get him excited for the game and prepared mentally to give his all.

This year I tried something different. Before one of his football games, we drove to the field with the music down, and I had the chance to speak with him about the game. I asked him what goal he wanted to accomplish during the game. He replied, "I want to have and/or be involved in five tackles and I want to score one touchdown." In that game he had to start as quarterback because the starting quarterback was out for some reason. During the game, he was involved in about ten tackles, scored one touchdown, and threw for one touchdown. Zyree did his thing that game. I was a proud father after that game.

I learned that Zyree does better with setting small goals leading to big accomplishments. Having intentional conversations before a big football game, a test, or a project in school as well as any life changes that he may have to experience.

In this letter, I want to share with you that learning something new is a chance to grow and expand yourself.

Learning something new!

As I told you before, I was given an opportunity to intern at a wonderful law firm in downtown Minneapolis, MN. While I was working there, I met many individuals who poured into my life and helped me in my journey. One person in particular who some would say, was a "big-time" attorney. I was told that this attorney would come into work about 6:00 a.m. every morning and that he had done so for the last ten or so years.

He said something to me that took my learning to a new level. So, one day I decided to stop by his office. I asked him, "Why do you show up to work every morning so early when there is no one to talk to?" Let me remind you this guy was a "big-time" lawyer, so for him to have a few minutes to speak with someone like me was pretty cool. The lawyer's response was by far one that took me by surprise. He replied, "So I can learn something new today." Then I asked him, "What do you mean?" He replied, "Every morning, I show up to work before everyone else so I can listen to the radio, read the newspaper, and watch the news. This enables me to stay up to date on things, keep my mind growing, and I am able to hold conversations with various people on different topics and concerns."

Hearing the lawyer speak on the importance of learning something new to share with others and to be able to hold conversations with different people, really changed my thinking and learning. I too started getting up early, turning on the news, reading the newspaper, and/or browsing through news websites, so that I could be knowledgeable about various topics and concerns that we face in our everyday lives. Doing this enhanced my understanding about things in life. It also helped me build relationships with many people I thought I wouldn't have, because I might not have understood certain things that they may have had a passion for. This also changed my mind about the importance of education and learning, which I will teach in the next chapter.

I want you to do the same. Get up every morning and watch the news. We both know that the news can sometimes be discouraging because of its negative views on things. However, those negative things can enhance your knowledge of those topics and maybe encourage you to do something. It can motivate you to do more research on what is going on so that you will know the full truth. Also, start reading the newspaper. Yes, news articles on your phone will suffice, but don't get misled, as not all outlets are true and correct. There is a lot of information to gather and I say get all you can. You will enjoy reading and it will become second nature. I say again, get a newspaper because you are physically holding it.

Newspapers may seem old school, but please try it, so you can get that feeling of reading the newspaper. Just reading things from various social media sites can sometimes confuse you because some of the information can be false and you will be doing more "fact-checking" than actual reading.

I know you probably really like reading about the NBA, NFL, and other professional sports. I love watching sports and conversing with others about who is going to win the finals, the

Super Bowl, or what is going on with the Olympics. Those conversations are fun too. However, knowing everything about sports and nothing else will only limit your conversation with the same people, which will eventually get boring. This is something that my grandmother often speaks to me about. Make sure to expand your knowledge. Expand your wisdom.

Learn about politics; learn about how to start a business. Learn about various educational avenues and learn about technology. Just learn so you can expand your mind and your understanding about things. You can never stop learning because the world will never stop teaching.

You got this young brother! Learning is a tool to change the world.

My challenge question to you:

What have you learned today? How will it help you in your life?

_____

_____

_____

_____

_____

_____

_____

_____

_____

_____

_____

_____

_____

_____

Remember, you can email me your response to mrrichardterrell@gmail.com.

To you, my young brother.
Richard D. Terrell

Letter 4

YOUR EDUCATION IS IMPORTANT!

"Education is the main ingredient to change this world."

-Richard D. Terrell-

Dear Young Brother,

This is my fourth letter to you. I hope you're having a wonderful time with whatever you are doing right now. We know that life can be tough. It can feel like everyone is against you, but it's not true. Some people really want to see you grow and use your education to make this world a better place.

I'm currently watching an interview with Dr. Shaquille O'Neal. Yes, he is a doctor. He was drafted to the NBA in 1992 as a 1st round and 1st pick overall by the Orlando Magic. He attended Louisiana State University and decided to leave after three years. He made a declaration to his mother that he would go back to get his bachelor's degree, which he did in 2000. Then in 2005, he graduated from the University of Phoenix and earned a Master's in Business Administration. After that, he wanted to continue his education and went on to Barry University where he earned a Doctorate of Education degree in Human Resources Development in 2012. Dr. O'Neal did all this while playing in the NBA.

I share this story because regardless of the path you decide to take, make sure you take furthering your education seriously.

Furthering your education does not necessarily mean you must attend college right after high school, because that may not work for you. You may decide to just go right into a certain career field, and that is okay. Just remember to always be a "Life-Long Learner." That is someone that is always learning wherever and whenever. Learning through conferences, trainings, online programs, reading books, etc. Education comes in different forms. Make sure to always recognize the importance of growth.

In the letter, I want to share with you the seriousness around the importance of education, your education!

Education is important!

While in elementary and middle school, I took my education as a joke. In other words, I thought my education was a game and I played around with it. While I was attending elementary school, I was probably the roughest student ever to attend Ramsey International Fine Arts School in Minneapolis, MN. I was always getting into some sort of altercation with other students and teachers. I would often show up to school and get sent back home because of something crazy I did. I did not take my education seriously.

The school got tired of my younger brother, Robert and I getting into trouble. They called a special meeting with my mother and grandmother and asked them to send us to a different school. If they didn't agree to do this, the school would expel us and force us to leave. So off we went to an alternative school, which was basically a school for students with behavioral issues, who got expelled from a regular school district. While attending the alternative school, I understood that I was just showing off and making a fool of myself for no reason. I wanted attention and I was using my negative behavior to seek negative attention, which in the long run hurt me. I felt like I didn't belong anywhere since Ramsey didn't want me. I knew that I needed to change something before I ended up spending some time somewhere I knew I could not handle. I knew that doing all those things for the wrong reasons had affected my educational development. It was time for a change.

I spent two years at the *alternative school. I felt like I needed that time to get my education back in order and get away from* certain things weighing me down. I knew that eventually I needed to take my education seriously. I remember seeing a quote on a poster by Malcolm X that said, "Education is the passport to the future, for tomorrow belongs to those who prepare for it today."

After seeing this, I was definitely motivated to use my education as a passport for the future, my future! I went on to graduate from the alternative school and attended Minneapolis North Community High School, in north Minneapolis, MN (Let's go Polars!!!) When entering high school, I had the mindset to stay focused on my education and to graduate on time. I had some ups and downs throughout the years, but I eventually graduated from high school on time. I was the first one in my family to attend college.

Let me tell you, my young brother, college was really hard for me. I attended my first year of college at North Dakota State University with a full ride scholarship because I was an African American student from the inner-city. That year was very tough on my family and me. I was stressed, depressed, and lost during that year because I was away from my family and didn't know what I was doing with myself. I lost my scholarship due to my G.P.A. being a 1.07, and the only class I passed was gym with a D. After losing my scholarship, I was forced to go home and attend a local community college to make up for some missing credits from the year before. After completing that year, I was ready to attend a bigger university to complete what I started. I went on to attend North Central University, a small Christian university in downtown Minneapolis, MN. I graduated in four years with a Bachelor of Science in Communications and a minor in Biblical Studies. Attending that school caused me to realize that I was bigger than my past actions and my past decisions.

Looking back, I realize that one must take their education seriously. If you don't, then others will not take you or your education. I know that some of you have made some educational mistakes before. You may have been suspended many times like I was; you may have messed up on exams. You may not have submitted your homework on time or missed many days of school. Do not let those things affect you or define you. I once allowed those things to define who I was.

Right now, from this moment on, learn from those mistakes and move forward with a different mindset, the growth mindset, be ready to achieve and make any necessary steps to build.

Honestly, your education is free unless you are attending a private school where your parents or guardians have to fund it. When you get into college, you may have to pay for it. Take advantage of the opportunity set before you. There is no need to show off for attention. There is no need to be the class clown and the center of attention. Don't be like me and wait until you get into high school or college to turn it around. You've got what it takes right now to do it.

Education is truly a gift in itself, and, unfortunately, it doesn't get the attention it deserves. We are taught that without a high school diploma, we can only look forward to a minimum wage job without advancement. Okay, what if you obtain your high school diploma? What about a college degree? This is the world informing you that education will increase your wealth out of school, but let's focus on the wealth of knowledge it instills in you that money cannot buy.

People cannot steal the wealth of your education and the knowledge it instills. If the world focused on the money that future student made, it would focus on keeping schools open by funding them. It would focus on paying teachers adequately to educate students to flourish out of school. Lastly, schools would be supplied equally throughout the U.S. Do not be blinded on the wealth garnered from graduating high school or a university but be determined to graduate and get all you can from school.

To see how important education is, you really have to look to the past. Education was not a right for everyone. In some places, being taught to read and write was illegal and punishable. Even when laws were made to counter this, schools were not equal. Schools were segregated. Unfortunately, black and brown schools did not have the funding for books and got the old, tattered edition of books. Schools desegregated and early on, youth had to walk to school while being shouted at, spit upon, and even hit—all to attend class. To get an education, they had to suffer through not being wanted, receiving threats, and some were even killed because of the color of their skin.

Looking into the past, you will see that African-Americans and other minority groups have some of the most brilliant minds. You will see a list of them fighting for education and driven to succeed. Even those who did not attend college right after high school but decided to further their education through a career path (hands-on experience), a trade, or a certification program. Unfortunately, you have to dig deep to learn that some of the biggest inventions were created by black and brown skinned people, where the world has highlighted others.

Education is truly the beginning of the big milestones you will face. Not only is your brain expanding as you grow, what you are taking in sets your future on fire. To not take full advantage of your education is a disservice to the people who fought for the right to freely learn in public. To be able to read and write your name is a blessing in itself, when some people weren't even afforded the chance to see their name printed before them. Education is a right and not a privilege, but you ultimately decide if you are going to attend school for the right or wrong reasons or not attend at all.

What will education or being a life-long learner do for me that I cannot do for myself? Honestly, if you are asking this question, I hope it's leading you back to the right path in your journey.

You are surrounded by people who have gotten where they are because of education and being a life-long learner. Education has given that businessman in your community the ability to not only open his store, but to stock it and gain a profit from the customers who come in. Education has given that professional banker the skills to help the store owner get a business loan. Education has given the man who owns the corner store the ability to obtain the services of an attorney to write up his business plan in order to apply for the business loan. Education has given that attorney the ability to do business law and contract law that will help others in the community.

Education has given your teacher the position to teach you. Education has given your school architect the capabilities to draw the blueprint in order for a construction company to build your school.

Education has given many professional athletes the ability to start businesses, create contracts, build partnerships with various businesses, and understand how business works.

Education will continue to give countless people abilities to do things that will change the world. Everywhere you turn, you will need educated individuals to help you achieve something you are unable to at first.

Education is a right and not a privilege. Once you realize that, your vision will become clearer. You're either opening the door to endless possibilities or closing it, but the choice ultimately is yours.

Here are some quotes on education:

"Education is the most powerful weapon which you can use to change the world."
Nelson Mandela

"The goal of education is the advancement of knowledge and the dissemination of truth."
John F. Kennedy

"You have to stay in school. You have to. You have to go to college. You have to get your degree. Because that's the one thing people can't take away from you is your education. And it is worth the investment."
Michelle Obama

"Education is the key to unlock the golden door of freedom."
George Washington Carver

My challenge question to you:

How will you use your education to better yourself and then others around you?

_____

_____

_____

_____

_____

_____

_____

_____

_____

_____

_____

_____

_____

_____

Remember, you can email me your response to mrrichardterrell@gmail.com.

To you, my young brother.
Richard D. Terrell

Letter 5

DRESSING FOR SUCCESS!

*"The way you dress can represent
who you are."*

-Richard D. Terrell-

Dear Young Brother,

This is my fifth letter to you. I hope things are coming together for you and that you are realizing that there is greatness in you.

In this letter, I want to share with you that dressing for success is and should be an everyday mission for you.

Dressing for Success!

While I was attending North Central University pursuing my degree in Communication, I was required to take a writing class and I wrote for our campus newspaper. During my time, I reported on various stories such as sports, opinions, and various other topics.

One particular article that I wrote in 2010 was titled, "Dress for Success!" In this article, I talked about how wearing business suits was truly a way to dress for success. The article discussed how wearing a suit is the new way to go and that others will not respect you if you do not wear some sort of professional attire. Now in 2019, I have to reintroduce my thoughts about this topic.

I love to wear suits. I love wearing suits with long ties and bow ties. That is my style. It makes me feel good when I have a suit on with a matching tie or a blazer with blue denim jeans. But for you, a suit may not be the way to go. You may feel like a suit is too old; it's not your style, and that is very understandable. Everyone can't pull off a suit and still feel good about themselves.

I would say that as a young man, you should always have a black and/or blue suit in your closet at all times. Those colors, including dark grey, are called "business colors." You will never know when you will be invited for an interview and need to wear one of those suits. You may be invited to attend a formal event that requires a suit. Believe me, you will need a suit in your closet, for a "just in case" moment.

I have come to understand that dressing for success has many definitions.

My definition of dressing for success is wearing something that makes you feel comfortable and good about yourself. If that means wearing a suit, please do it. Wear it well and feel great about it. If that means wearing some jeans and some Jordans, please do it. If it means wearing some True Religion jeans (I don't know if you all still wear those types of jeans) and some Kyries, Lebrons, or Currys, please do it. A blazer jacket with some Polo shoes, please do it. Wear it well and feel great about it.

When you are dressing for success, make sure that you wear things that are appropriate and acceptable for the environment that you are in. Young brother, if you are sagging when you have something nice on, please stop doing that. It is nasty and very disrespectful. Others shouldn't be able to see the clothes under your pants. You are much better than that. Also, it is very important that you understand personal hygiene. Make sure that you are taking showers, brushing your teeth, and wearing deodorant and cologne. I do not care to see the color or pattern of a young brother's drawers and neither do others. I do not find it appealing. There is no appropriate place where sagging would be acceptable. I also cannot comprehend having to pull up my pants to drop them down again, or one actually wearing a belt, but your buttocks are still in plain view.

I am a fan of looking back in history, because honestly it's the best way to see how far we have come in a specific area. So, let me go back to where sagging all began. It began in prison. And was later transformed and adapted into our culture. When inmates were given uniforms, they were given pants that were too large and belts were not allowed for obvious reasons, so sagging began. Sagging throughout its years has been tied to three types of people—prisoners, rappers, and gang members. Sagging became more embraced and still is a style for today but holds no positive connotation.

Looking forward, yes, we will always be judged by the outside before people get to know who we truly are. And, yes, it takes the effort of the other person to want to get to know you better. If you are confident in yourself, you're already opening the door to be approached. Be confident through your mind, body, and soul. I can be confident in a $75 suit or a $300 suit. The price means nothing; it is all about how you carry yourself.

Dressing for yourself also shows how you carry yourself. If I am running to the store, I would likely throw on a sweat suit, something comfortable for running around. Dressing for yourself has more to do with you, yourself, and your style. Know that no one can outdo *you* more than yourself, no matter how hard they try. You also cannot mimic a celebrity to be like them when you are you. I want you to be secure in yourself and dress for yourself.

Dressing for success starts with you. Are you ready to feel good about yourself? Are you ready for a change in the way you present yourself? I hope so! You've got this! I believe in you!

My challenge question to you:

How will you dress for success?

_____

_____

_____

_____

_____

_____

_____

_____

_____

_____

_____

_____

_____

_____

_____

_____

_____

Remember, you can email me your response to mrrichardterrell@gmail.com.

To you, my young brother.
Richard D. Terrell

Section 2

YOU ARE STRONG

My definition of STRONG

Successful

Thankful

Remarkable

Ordinary

Natural

Gifted

Letter 6

TRAVEL FOR FUN!

"Travel, see the world"

-Richard D. Terrell-

Dear Young Brother,

This is my sixth letter to you. I hope you are having a wonderful time reading and engaging in this content. I'm having fun writing this to you in hopes that you are receiving something from it.

I'm currently browsing through my old photos, and I came across my first trip abroad, which was to Ghana in Africa. (I often reminisce about this trip). The trip to Ghana was a life-changing experience. I was able to see Ghana through my own eyes and not what they show on television. I was able to visit two former slave castles, Elmina Castle and Cape Coast Castle, the first president of Ghana, Kwame Nkrumah Memorial Site, W.E.B. Du Bois Memorial Site, the University of Ghana, a small, yet powerful and loving community called Senchi Ferry. The trip was amazing. Ghana was very family oriented and loving. They showed us so much love and they appreciated us for coming to visit. I cannot wait until I am able to visit there again.

Travel for fun!

I have traveled to Washington State, Washington, DC, North Dakota, Texas, California, Iowa, Wisconsin, Missouri, Mississippi,

Alabama, Louisiana, Georgia, Tennessee Virginia, Pennsylvania, New York, Maryland, Florida, West Virginia, the Bahamas, and Ghana, Yes, I have been to all those places and will be traveling to other states in the near future. I also hope to be traveling out of the country sooner rather than later. I really want to travel to Ethiopia, Egypt, and South America because of their rich history, the pyramids, Nelson Mandela, and the Nile River. I love to travel, especially with people that enjoy traveling too.

I have traveled for family vacations, family reunions, basketball games, tournaments for pleasure, and business.

Every time I travel, I make sure to check out their local African American community, and I try to experience something they have there that I don't have back home in Minnesota. For example, I like to eat at a unique restaurant or visit a church to worship and fellowship with people there. I usually find myself trying to relate to how the people in that particular community feel.

Make sure you travel and see the world. The world is much larger than what you see in your community and neighborhood. Travel so that you can witness how others live in different states and countries. Try living the way they live so you can better understand different cultures, beliefs, and customs. My grandma often tells me, "Boy, you got to travel. Go see the world and see everything that it has to offer you."

Travel with a purpose. When you travel with a purpose, you are more likely to accomplish the goal in getting to where you want to go and exploring. Do your research on how you will travel. There are different modes of transportation to fit anyone's budget. Get your family involved. If your parents have not left the state, you are most likely not going to leave the state out of comfort. My family opened doors that made it possible for us to visit other states, mainly to see family. Begin speaking to your family about traveling outside your state for a mini-trip or a vacation. Show them that you have done your research and that it is important for you to visit that special place. Make it a goal to complete.

One of my favorite places to visit is Washington, DC. I enjoy visiting the National Museum of African History and Culture, Dr. Martin Luther King, Jr memorial, Howard University, etc. I actually interned in Washington, DC on the United States Capitol Hill with a House Representative through an Adoption and Foster Care Organization in 2011. I also attended the Million Man March in 2015.

Take advantage of opportunities at your school, church, and extra-curricular activities that are offered that may allow you to travel. There have been study abroad opportunities at my university that I have taken advantage of. Traveling will enable you to learn from their rich history and culture. Traveling should be fun! You should be able to enjoy yourself in a new environment, wherever you go.

Before you go to a new place, make sure you ask yourself, "What do I want to get out of this trip?" After the trip, you should be able to look back and answer these questions: Did this trip serve its purpose? Did I get out of my comfort zone during the trip? What did the community sound like, smell like, and look like? Did I feel welcomed there? Would I go back to visit again?

These are some of the questions I had to ask myself when I got back from visiting Ghana.

So, now I am telling you, Travel! See the world! Experience life outside of your community!

My challenge question to you:

Where will your next trip be?

_____

_____

_____

_____

_____

_____

_____

_____

_____

_____

_____

_____

_____

Remember, you can email me your response to mrrichardterrell@gmail.com.

To you, my young brother.
Richard D. Terrell

Letter 7

TAKE ADVANTAGE OF EVERY OPPORTUNITY!

"Many opportunities only come once, so seize the opportunity when it comes."

-Richard D. Terrell-

Dear Young Brother,

This is my seventh letter to you. Right now, I am just thinking about how life gives us many chances to try to make things better for ourselves and the community.

One of my favorite episodes of *Shark Tank* was season 14, episode 22, where a black entrepreneur presented an amazing business to the sharks around a clothing brand to increase awareness to the Historical Black College and Universities (HBCU). She was grilled by the Sharks. However, she stayed focused and continued with her business, purpose, and calling to do something great.

I couldn't help but think about how many of us miss opportunities like this because we hesitate or don't act when moments come our way. This episode serves as a reminder that success often comes down to seizing the right opportunity at just the right time.

For this reason, I am writing this letter about seizing that opportunity when it comes your way.

Taking advantage of every opportunity!

Today, I heard a song by a Washington, D.C. rapper named Wale. Wale was given an opportunity to sign under the Rick Ross label, Maybach Music Group. He took advantage of the opportunity and went for it all. Now he is probably one of the most influential rappers out there. As I did some research on Wale, I came across this quote, "If I woke up tomorrow and didn't have a dollar, as long as I have my heart, I can get it all over."

If you just read this quote a few times in your head, you will see how powerful this man is with his lyrics. This quote basically talks about you waking up every morning and seizing the opportunity that you currently have. No matter what you did yesterday, a month ago or even a year ago, don't worry; you have been given another opportunity to get it right and move forward and take advantage of this day.

In 2016, I started a program that I have been working on for many years. I knew I was able to do it; I just needed the timing to be right and to make sure that it all worked out to better serve the individuals I was working with. I spent many years trying to figure this thing out—how it would work out or if it would work at all. Let me be honest with you, when I was approached about the opportunity, I was very sad and was going to say no. But I realized that I prepared myself for something like this for many years and it was my time now. After prayer, I came to the realization that this is the opportunity I've been waiting on. I finally said yes to starting my program.

The program I started is called R.E.A.L. Leaders (Reaching Everyone's Achievable Limits). This program focuses on leadership development, social awareness, self-identity, academic enrichment, and service learning for young men of color. Also, the program focuses on building brotherhood between young men of color and what is essential in today's society.

The mission of R.E.A.L. (Reaching Everyone's Achievable Limits) Leaders is to provide young men from diverse backgrounds with the opportunities to learn the necessary skills and awareness to become vision and goal centered, positively focused, productive, and determined to succeed. We will achieve this mission through academic enrichment and excellence, leadership development, and an increase of self-identity and social awareness.

The vision for R.E.A.L. Leaders is to provide opportunities for young men from diverse backgrounds to develop the social and academic skills needed to enable them to become the next generation of great leaders in their families, communities, and the world. Through their leadership, we hope to change the stereotypes of young men of color and build bridges of understanding between diverse communities.

This is one out of many opportunities that have been given to me. Now with this opportunity, I am able to speak, motivate, inspire, encourage, and empower young men in all areas while sharing my program with others.

Take advantage of opportunities when you can. If you have an opportunity to be on a basketball team, consider doing it because you don't know where that might take you. If it is working a job where you can build up your social and leadership skills, taking it can lead to additional possibilities. If it is being a part of a school group such as the chess club or the debate team, that experience may open further doors for you. If it is going on a family trip to wherever, take it if you can, because you don't know what you will learn from the experience.

Opportunities don't always come at the best time, and you will not always have a door opened when you feel ready. Some opportunities even have an expiration date, which you need to commit to or not during a given time frame. Some opportunities will lead you one step closer to your dream and it's all about taking that next step towards your purpose. This is why you have to be okay with getting uncomfortable. Seizing an opportunity sometimes will get you out of your comfort zone, which is good. Challenge yourself to seize an opportunity to bring you closer to your dream.

I also do not believe that you should take every opportunity that comes your way. You should be secure in yourself and ask yourself questions prior to taking or not taking an opportunity. Like I said before, I pray over everything before making a decision. I cannot in good conscience, not speak to God before ultimately making a decision. I believe you should speak to your higher being or your closest confidant, as not everyone needs to know your every move prior to deciding. An opportunity will not distract you, but it will uplift you and carry you higher. If an opportunity is taking you away, re-evaluate where you are going and think of the possibility that you could be being directed down a new path. Otherwise, it is a distraction to say no to. An opportunity will lift you, not hinder you.

Take advantage of everything! You got this!

My challenge question to you:

What opportunity will you take advantage of next?

_____

_____

_____

_____

_____

_____

_____

_____

_____

_____

_____

_____

_____

_____

Remember, you can email me your response to mrrichardterrell@gmail.com.

To you, my young brother.
Richard D. Terrell

Letter 8

SPORTS IS MORE THAN JUST THE GAME!

"Basketball and Football are more than a sport you play on the court or field."

-Richard D. Terrell-

Dear Young Brother,

This is my eighth letter to you. I hope things are going well for you and your family, and that things are heading the right way for you.

I was just looking at one of my basketball photos from when I played basketball for North Central University in Minneapolis, MN, a small Division 3 private school in our downtown area. We were the Rams!

I had hopes of going to the NBA or the NFL just like many of you. However, attending North Central University, I quickly realized that *sports are more than just the game itself.* It's about the lessons learned, the challenges faced, and personal growth through the process that comes from pushing yourself beyond your limits. I learned this personally during my time playing college basketball at North Central University. I went into each game thinking it was about the scoreboard and winning every game and really embarrassing the "opps." The true value of sports lies in the experiences off the court and field.

In this letter, I want to share with you some key lessons I have learned through basketball that shaped me into who I am today.

Sports are more than just a game!

Growing up, I played a lot of sports. I played basketball, football, ran track, and even tried playing baseball for one season. To be completely honest with you, it wasn't until college that I realized that basketball is more than just running up and down the court, trying to score or that football was more than running down the field trying to score on the opposite team. So, I want to share with you my story about how I used sports as a means to build up my communication, leadership skills, and confidence. Also, how you too, can do the same.

There are many professional athletes that have said the same thing. Look at the list below:

"When I step on that basketball court, I'm thinking about basketball. I'm thinking about winning, but there's so much that goes into the thought about how I'm going to open this game up to others. It's so much more than just basketball.
- Carmelo Anthony

"I have to tell you, I'm proudest of my life off the court. There will always be great basketball players who bounce that little round ball, but my proudest moments are affecting people's lives, effecting change, and being a role model in the community."
- Magic Johnson

"I think for me, or for anyone who plays the quarterback position, it's almost an unspoken word when you think about leadership. Some guys can be a leader and be a running back or a lineman, or wide receiver, strong safety, or linebacker. But

when you speak of quarterbacks, it's automatically a default that you're supposed to be a leader."
- Cam Newton

"Everyone made an impact in their own way last game. This is a team game and it takes the whole team to get the win."
- Odell Beckham Jr.

Each quote has a different meaning as to why sports show and bring out things other than winning a game. While I played sports at the recreational center, I used sports as a way to get girls, receive some cool points from my boys and people around the community. I thought I was doing my thing growing up, playing basketball. I thought I was the best at playing basketball. I could probably beat you one-on-one. LOL.

Playing college basketball helped me develop some skills that I could use in my everyday life, and I would like to share them with you—communication, leadership skills, teamwork and confidence.

Effective Communication:

Playing basketball, my coach had always forced his players to talk. Every time we would get on the court we had to talk to each other. If we were calling a play, we had to communicate. If we were playing the ball or someone was open, we had to communicate. Remember the saying, "A closed mouth, don't get fed." That rings true with basketball. Now I must communicate with individuals I come in contact with. True communication comes face-to-face, not through Instant Messenger or texting. I get a lot done by just communicating with others.

Leadership:

Being a point guard, I had to lead the team. If I were off that night, then the team would have to pick up the slack or they would be off as well. I had to make sure I came to practice ready to be challenged and ready to go for it all. Every time I got in the game, my teammates would need to know what to do, how, and why to do it. I was the leader.

Collaboration/Teamwork:

Being on a team teaches you how to work together in all aspects. Making sure you're on-time to practice together, making sure that you're leading by example together, and ensuring that no one falls behind if they are struggling to keep up or maintain. There is a saying from an African Proverb that is so true in this society. "If you want to go fast, go alone. If you want to go far, go together."

Building confidence:

Through playing basketball, my confidence grew because I was challenged to think outside the box, and in how to accept criticism. Playing basketball opened my eyes to know why my coach challenged me every day on the court. He saw something more in me than I could see in myself. He saw that I needed someone to push me to the next level. I needed someone to encourage me, inspire me, and empower me.

Most CEOs or presidents of large companies played a sport in either high school and/or college. Do some research!!!

My challenge question to you:

How would you use the sport you love to play to change the world?

_____

_____

_____

_____

_____

_____

_____

_____

_____

_____

_____

_____

_____

_____

Remember, you can email me your response to mrrichardterrell@gmail.com.

To you, my young brother.
Richard D. Terrell

Letter 9

BUILD YOUR NETWORK!

"Knowing someone will sometimes get you further in life than knowing how to get there."

-Richard D. Terrell-

Dear Young Brother,

This is my ninth letter to you. I hope you are doing great. As for me, I am just sitting here thinking about life and the saying, "It's not what you know; it's who you know."

One of the most valuable things I have learned in life is that success is rarely achieved alone, and it is often the result of the connections you have and the people we have surrounded ourselves with in our lives.

Building a strong network has been a key part of my journey, and it is something that I wish I had known as a younger man. Whether it is mentors, coaches, teammates, friends, or community members, the relationships you cultivate can open doors and new opportunities that can help you grow in more areas than you ever imagined.

In this letter, I want to share why building your network is essential and how the right connections can truly make a difference in shaping your future.

Build up your network!

I know you have heard that saying before. It is so true! Some of my greatest accomplishments came because I knew the right person to get me there.

I went on my first college tour my sophomore year of high school to Chicago and my junior year to Atlanta because I knew someone who ran the program that was taking students to visit colleges.

When I got the opportunity to intern at the law firm in downtown Minneapolis, MN, I knew the right person who was placing students in internships.

When I received a full-ride scholarship to North Dakota State University, I knew someone there to help me get in.

When I went to Atlanta, GA for a young preacher's conference, I knew someone that had attended the conference the year before who connected me to the program manager.

When I attended a church conference in Illinois, I knew the person who was the president over the youth department there.

When I was given the opportunity to work at a school for the first time, I knew the person who was running the school.

When I started my R.E.A.L. Leaders program, I knew a few people that were very interested in meeting with me to learn more about the program and the possibility of having the program at their school.

When I got my school principal license, I knew a few people who could get me a job in a school.

Your network and connections can get you far in life if you allow them to. It is one thing meeting people on social media like Facebook, LinkedIn, Instagram, and Snapchat.

However, it's another thing to actually stay in contact with those people and check on them once in a while.

My son often says, "Dad, you know a lot of people." It is so true. Everywhere we go, I have to say I know someone there. For the most part, I know most people off the social media sites because I make it my duty to check in with individuals, I care to build a relationship with. I also make sure I attend networking events through the city to meet people outside of my area. If you like basketball, try meeting someone that loves football. If you love business, try meeting someone that loves politics. If you like food, try meeting someone that loves chess. Do it and see where this relationship takes you.

Make it a goal to get to know people who are outside of your comfort zone. Reach out to them, check on them, and see how they are doing. Find ways to use your network to build. I remember people telling me all the time that people are in your life for a reason and you must find out why they are in your life.

Building your network also means understanding that not everyone needs a place in your life. Sometimes we get so caught up in knowing everyone, and we don't realize that some people can be a distraction. People should not take more energy from you than they are giving. If someone constantly wants something from you but you never hear from them until they need something, it's time for you to remove them from your circle. I believe you have family, best friends, friends, and social interactions. If you do not know how to end a friendship, that's fine, but know your boundaries.

Go for it! Build your network!

My challenge question to you:

Who have you connected with today? How will that network help you?

_____

_____

_____

_____

_____

_____

_____

_____

_____

_____

_____

_____

_____

Remember, you can email me your response to mrrichardterrell@gmail.com.

To you, my young brother.
Richard D. Terrell

Section 3

YOU ARE POWERFUL

My definition of POWERFUL

Productive

Obedient

Well-made

Entertaining

Responsible

Faithful

Unique

Likeable

Letter 10

LEADERSHIP IS IN YOU!

"You have what it takes to be a great leader."

-Richard D. Terrell-

Dear Young Brother,

This is my tenth letter to you. I hope things are going well for you and whatever you are doing. I also hope that you are having fun and enjoying yourself. Remember that your happiness comes from within. I remember sitting back and asking myself on many occasions why many look to me for help and guidance? I then realized that I am a leader; and my leadership goes beyond my family.

Leadership isn't about the titles or positions; it's about the ability to inspire, motivate, empower, and encourage others to move forward with the same mission and vision. True leadership isn't something that is given to you; it's something that comes within.

My own journey with leadership was built with self confidence, integrity, and taking responsibility for my actions and the motivation to do something to make a difference.

In this letter, I want to remind you that the leader you are searching for is already in you. It is up to you to cultivate it, trust in it, and step into one day at a time. Believe in the lead, in you!

Leadership in you!

Everyone has leadership abilities and skills. Everyone is truly born with some sort of understanding or knowledge about leadership. If it is guiding and leading others to be a success, speaking greatness into people's lives, or just supporting others in a vision, these are all aspects of leadership. You do not have to be the center of attention and your name does not have to be the first at the top of the paper in order to be a great leader. Leadership comes in different forms.

I love this quote from LeBron James,

> My game is really played above time. I don't say that like I'm saying I'm ahead of my time. I'm saying, like, if I'm on the court and I throw a pass, the ball that I've thrown will lead my teammate right where he needs to go, before he even knows that that's the right place to go to.

After reading this quote, I noticed that LeBron James has a visionary leadership style. He prepares his team to be better and prepares them to press and push forward in order to be great.

I remember growing up; I had many opportunities to showcase my leadership. I've led my basketball team to a win; I've led groups of adults in conversations and discussions. I've led my classmates in a group presentation. I've had experience leading my church and various churches in expanding their spiritual walk, and I've helped a group of students improve their leadership skills.

You will find yourself leading in different areas of your life. You can lead when you are hanging out with your friends, playing sports, in school, at your job, speaking with people, and just chilling alone. Your leadership skills must continue to grow too.

To become a leader, you will have to break out of your shell. You will need to use your talents and gifts. If you are shy, this may be very hard, as it is easier to follow than to lead. If you have a big idea, take the right step towards completing it and make it happen. Don't be afraid to speak up, because you're concerned with how others may react. You will never know the outcome of an idea if you sit on it. If you are used to being in the back seat, take the front seat for a while and be brave to offer up your ideas. This will also build your confidence in more leadership roles. Not everyone is meant to lead in all things. But you will realize that you have to take on some leadership roles and you need to be comfortable doing it

Here are ways to expand and grow your leadership skills:

1. Be a good example for others.
2. Continue to encourage activities by working together.
3. Focus on pressing forward.
4. Focus on making decisions together as a team.
5. Practice confident communication.
6. Create a vision board for yourself.
7. Create a planner for yourself.
8. Set goals.
9. Mentor others younger than you.

I hope this list will help you in building up your leadership skills.

My challenge question to you:

How will you build up your leadership skills?

_____

_____

_____

_____

_____

_____

_____

_____

_____

_____

_____

_____

_____

_____

Remember, you can email me your response to mrrichardterrell@gmail.com.

To you, my young brother.
Richard D. Terrell

Letter 11

KNOW YOUR HISTORY!

*"History goes beyond just knowing
the popular figures."*

-Richard D. Terrell-

Dear Young Brother,

This is my eleventh letter to you. I hope things are going well for you and that you continue to be happy with life.

Understanding your history goes beyond just simply knowing the public figures, which is always good. However, I have learned that connecting with the broader story of your ancestors, your culture, and the experiences that shaped who you are today.

Learning about the past, we not only gain a deeper appreciation for where we come from but also find strength and perspective for where we can go.

In this letter, I want to encourage you to explore and seek your history; learn about the stories, the struggles, and triumphs of those who came before you. Knowing your history will help you move forward in life with confidence, purpose, and pride.

Know your history!

I remember my grandma always talked about how history is important. She said that I must understand my history because if

I don't, then I would repeat it. It's very important that you know your family history. Ask yourself these questions:

Where did my family migrate from?

What are my family's traditions?

What is my family's favorite recipe?

Where did my family get its last name?

Who is my great grandmother, my great-great grandmother, and my great-great-great grandmother?

Also, knowing your race history is very important as well. I am talking about knowing more than just the normal individuals that your school speaks about or you study about.

I love hearing about the late Dr. Martin Luther King, Jr., Malcolm X, Mrs. Rosa Parks, Harriet Tubman, and Barack Obama. These individuals did some amazing things. There are also others that are a part of our history, such as Booker T. Washington, George Washington Carver, WEB Dubois, Joe Louis, Sojourner Truth, Benjamin E. Mays, Roy Wilkins, Carter G. Woodson, etc.

I love African American history so much that every time I travel, I have to visit some museums or centers that may have some artifacts about African American history. History has created you and will continue to do so. Through many ups and downs, trials and tribulations, reading your history will definitely keep you moving forward and enduring through it all.

Do you know that Rosa Parks was not the first person who refused to get up? Do you know she was not the first person to initiate a boycott of riding the bus? Do you know that behind every major influential and powerful civil rights leader, there are literally ten plus people who have had the same story? It's easy to focus on one person, but it's a lie to think that one person is the sole reason for the change. Many people continue to come together for one dream, and it's our duty to learn about the countless people who also put that dream together.

You have to look back to see how far we have come as a people and as a world. You are not the same yesterday and you should not remain the same. That is the same with history. History is always changing, and you will realize sometimes that it isn't changing for the better. Some things happen again years later, or it may feel like we are going more backwards than forward. You may not be able to change the world by yourself, but the beauty is that you will come together with other people who feel the same as you to bring about a change.

How will you leave your mark on the world? What do you want your legacy to be? Do you know that you are already on track to make history because many people before you have paved the way?

I love this quote by the Late Dr. Martin Luther King, Jr.

"We are not makers of history. We are made by history."

My challenge question to you:

How would you describe your history?

_____

_____

_____

_____

_____

_____

_____

_____

_____

_____

_____

_____

_____

_____

Remember, you can email me your response to mrrichardterrell@gmail.com.

To you, my young brother.
Richard D. Terrell

Letter 12

IT IS OKAY TO BE DIFFERENT!

"Yes, you are different."

-Richard D. Terrell-

Dear Young Brother,

This is my twelfth letter to you. I hope you are enjoying these letters.

Being different is not just okay; it should and will be something to be celebrated. Growing up, I sometimes felt the pressure to fit in or follow the crowd, but I knew I was different from others. I know that the qualities that make me unique are actually my greatest strengths.

In a world where everyone is trying to be the same, standing out and embracing what makes you different can be powerful. In this letter, I want to let you know that it is not only okay to be different, but it is also the very thing that will help you in your own path.

It is okay to be different!

As I thought about the title for this letter, "It is okay to be different," I thought about the song by 2 Chainz—"I'm different! I'm different. Yeah, I'm different." I did a message on this title at a church for the youth service. It was quite fun because I had a few young people singing the song and talking to each other about going home to listen to it.

Everyone is different in their own way. Let me tell you a little about how I grew up feeling different. During my elementary school years, it was really hard for me to speak. I would sound out certain words in a way that others wouldn't understand and they would just laugh at me. I was very bothered by it, so I started to avoid talking to people. Even to this day, I see myself messaging, emailing, and texting more because I prefer not to speak if I can avoid it. I knew I was different. At first, I wanted to fit in with the crowd by trying to talk like others and be someone I wasn't. Then a few years ago, I realized that I was born this way for a reason and that I shouldn't be ashamed of the way I talk because I'm amazing just the way I am.

Now I use my struggles from the past to my advantage, by speaking and helping those that may be struggling with the same thing. When I have to speak in front of a crowd, I make sure to tell a funny story or crack a joke so I can feel more comfortable once I actually get into my message.

Embrace your differences as part of who you are. It will help you not to be ashamed, and it will keep you from conforming to another mold. Everyone has differences, whether they acknowledge it or not. No two people are the same, and if they were, what fun would that be?

Young brother, you may feel that you must be with the "in" crowd, but it is okay to be different. Standing out only gives you more ability to be the person you are meant to be and no one else.

It is okay to be different!
  You are different!
  Your thoughts are different!
  Your skills are different!
  Your goals are different!
  Your mindset is different!

The way you act is different!
The way you smile is different!
The way you laugh is different! The
way you write is different!
The way you dress is different!
The way you play sports is different!
The way you look is different!
You are different!
Remember that!

My challenge question to you:

How will you stand out from the crowd?

_____

_____

_____

_____

_____

_____

_____

_____

_____

_____

_____

_____

_____

_____

_____

Remember, you can email me your response to mrrichardterrell@gmail.com.

To you, my young brother.
Richard D. Terrell

Letter 13

KNOW YOUR WORTH!

"Your worth is an inside job."

-Richard D. Terrell-

Dear Young Brother,

This is my thirteenth letter to you. I hope you are enjoying these letters as much as I am enjoying writing them to you.

As you grow older, you will encounter many challenges and experiences that may make you question who you are or where you are heading. You might face moments of doubt, guilt, or regret, and sometimes it will feel like you are not measuring up to others. But I want you to know that with all your heart, mind, and body that your worth is not determined by comparing yourself or achievements. You do not need to be like others to be of importance. The world can try to tell you something different, but you are special.

In this letter, I want to share with you the importance of knowing your worth and not allowing others to define you and create you into something you are not.

Know your worth!

You are unique; you are worth more than what society tries to pour into you. The way you think, the way you laugh, the way you dream. Those are things that make you who you are. There will always be someone who may be faster, smarter, or even more successful at times. That does not take away from you, your worth and what you bring to the table.

Your journey is your path. It will unfold in its own time; and it may not come when you want it to, but it will come. Growth does not come overnight or all at once. It happens in time and slowly— one day at a time, and one step at a time.

You will make mistakes, and that is okay. You will stumble; that is okay. You may not have everything figured out just yet. That is how we learn and how we grow. It is part of being a human, being a young man. What really matters is that you do not give up on yourself or your process. Keep pushing! Keep learning and most importantly, keep believing in yourself and your worth!

Remember, you do not have to be perfect; you just have to be you, and that is already good enough. Whether you are in school, playing sports, or just figuring out who you want to become, know you are worthy of everything. You are capable of much more than you may currently realize. The key is to trust yourself!

I believe in you more than you think, even if I don't know you personally. You have so much potential, and I am so proud of the young man you are becoming. Your family, this community, and this world need what only you can offer. You are meant for greatness. Enjoy your journey, embrace the challenges, and remember your growth is not about being perfect; it's about becoming the best version of yourself.

Know your worth!

Never let anyone or anything make you feel like you are less than!

You are worthy of love!

You are worthy of success!

You are worthy of everything your heart desires!

My challenge question to you:

Do you know your worth? What can you do to start realizing your worth?

_____

_____

_____

_____

_____

_____

_____

_____

_____

_____

_____

_____

_____

_____

_____

Remember, you can email me your response to mrrichardterrell@gmail.com.

To you, my young brother.
Richard D. Terrell

Letter 14

TRUST YOUR PROCESS!

*"Your process is your process, and
some people will not understand it."*

-Richard D. Terrell-

Dear Young Brother,

This is my last letter to you in this book. Keep embracing you!

It is important that as you continue to grow, chase your dreams, and become a better version of yourself that you learn to TRUST YOUR PROCESS!

When I mentor young men in the community, I often have to share with them to slow down and take it easy. They are so quick to make fast decisions based on their current emotions instead of thinking through those things and figuring out ways to accomplish that goal or dream.

I share another part of me with you; this book was originally published for you back in 2018. But I wasn't ready to release it to the public due to my insecurities, my lack of confidence, and understanding of self.

In this letter, I want to share that trusting your process and your journey is the only way!

Trust your Process!
In life, we often feel the pressure to have everything figured out,

to be perfect right from the start. There is no set timeline for success or happiness, and there is no need to rush that.

The process you are going through right now, at this moment, is where you need to be. It may not always feel like it, and sometimes it might seem like things are not moving in the right or perfect direction. Sometimes things may be moving slowly or not at all. The saying "Everything happens for a reason" is a true statement. We don't always understand why it happens, but when that time comes, it reveals itself to you.

Trust every step, no matter how big or small, good or bad, trials and tribulations. There will be times when you want to give up or feel like it is not paying off to your liking. Maybe you wonder if it is all worth it but remember, trust your process!

With your effort, your dedication, and your patience, it will definitely pay off. Keep trusting that the small steps you are taking, every single day, will lead to the big things as you continue this journey. Life is a journey of constant growth and change, and some days will be easier than others; some days may feel like you are not going anywhere. On other days, it may feel like you cannot see the light at the end of the tunnel. Those moments and experiences are a part of your process.

I am proud of the progress you have made and the effort you continue to put in during your journey.

Keep your head up!
Stay focused on your goals and dreams!
Trust your process!

My challenge question to you:

What does "process" mean to you?

_____

_____

_____

_____

_____

_____

_____

_____

_____

_____

_____

_____

_____

Remember, you can email me your response to mrrichardterrell@gmail.com.

To you, my young brother.
Richard D. Terrell

MY CHALLENGE TO YOU YOUNG BROTHER!

I challenge you, my young brother… To find your purpose through the One that created you, the One that has already created a path for you and the One that has created you to do great things on this earth.

I challenge you, my young brother… To always put education first. Use your education to change, shape and build this world.

I challenge you, my young brother… To pursue some sort of college or higher education. College is definitely in your future.

I challenge you, my young brother… To learn something new every single day. Learn something that will help you in your day-to-day activities.

I challenge you, my young brother… To travel the world, see everything.

I challenge you, my young brother… To take advantage of any opportunity that presents itself to you.

I challenge you, my young brother… To say to yourself every morning, "I am somebody."

I challenge you, my young brother…. To dress the way, you want people to know and respect you as.

I challenge you, my young brother…. To not only use sports as an activity but use it to keep yourself physically fit.

I challenge you, my young brother… To understand that you are a leader.

I challenge you, my young brother… To know who you are and what you are becoming.

I challenge you, my young brother… To know your history and understand that our ancestors have done remarkable things for us.

I challenge you, my young brother… To know and understand that money doesn't make you powerful, doesn't make you rich and doesn't make you more popular.

I challenge you, my young brother… To stand out of the crowd. I dare you to be different because it is okay.

There is HOPE!

How will you challenge yourself to improve, grow, and become the best version of yourself?

_____

_____

_____

_____

_____

There is Hope…

www.ingramcontent.com/pod-product-compliance
Lightning Source LLC
Chambersburg PA
CBHW021126130626
46554CB00002B/886